P9-ARD-774

A Parade of Animal Poems

JUMPETY-BUMPETY HOP

Kay Chorao

Baby's First Book Club

ACKNOWLEDGMENTS

"Moon," from *Laughing Time: Collected Nonsense* by William Jay Smith. Copyright © 1990 by William Jay Smith. Reprinted by permission of Farrar, Straus & Giroux, Inc. "Brothers," copyright © 1978 by William Cole. First appeared in *An Arkful of Animals,* published by Houghton Mifflin Company. Reprinted by permission of Curtis Brown, Ltd., and Houghton Mifflin Company. All rights reserved. "The Old Woman," from *Appley Dapply's Nursery Rhymes* by Beatrix Potter. Copyright © 1917 by Frederick Warne & Co., London. Reprinted by permission of Frederick Warne & Co. "Mice," from *Fifty-one New Nursery Rhymes* by Rose Fyleman. Copyright © 1931, 1932 by Doubleday, a division of Bantam Doubleday Dell Publishing Group, Inc. Reprinted by permission of Doubleday, a division of Bantam Doubleday Dell Publishing Group, Inc., and The Society of Authors as the literary representative of the Estate of Rose Fyleman. "The Sea Gull," by Leroy F. Jackson. Copyright © 1996 by Rand McNally. All rights reserved. "The Prayer of the Little Ducks," from *Prayers from the Ark* by Carmen Bernos de Gasztold, translated by Rumer Godden, translation copyright © 1962, renewed 1990 by Rumer Godden. Original copyright © 1947, copyright © 1955 by Editions du Cloitre. Used by permission of Viking Penguin, a division of Penguin Books USA Inc., and Curtis Brown, Ltd., as the literary representative of the Estate of Rumer Godden. "The Duck," from *Verses from 1929 On* by Ogden Nash. Copyright © 1936 by Ogden Nash. First appeared in *The Saturday Evening Post.* Used by permission of Little, Brown and Company. "Tom's Little Dog," by Walter de la Mare. Reprinted by permission of The Literary Trustees of Walter de la Mare, and The Society of Authors as their representative. "The Rabbit," from *Under the Tree* by Elizabeth Madox Roberts. Copyright © 1922 by B. W. Huebsch, Inc., renewed 1950 by Ivor S. Roberts. Copyright © 1930 by Viking Penguin, Inc., renewed copyright © 1958 by Ivor S. Roberts. Used by permission of Viking Penguin, a division of Penguin Books USA Inc. "Grandfather Frog," by Louise Seaman Bechtel. From *Another Here and Now Story Book,* edited by Lucy Sprague Mitchell. Copyright © 1937 by E. P. Dutton, renewed copyright © 1965 by Lucy Sprague Mitchell. Used by permission of Dutton Children's Books, a division of Penguin Books USA Inc. "The Polliwog," from *Wildwood Fables* by Arthur Guiterman, copyright © 1927 by E. P. Dutton and Company. Reprinted by permission of Louise H. Sclove. "The Little Turtle," from *The Collected Poems of Vachel Lindsay.* Copyright © 1920 by Macmillan Publishing Company, renewed 1948 by Elizabeth C. Lindsay. "The Pum Na-Na Frogs," by John Lyons. From *A Caribbean Dozen,* edited by John Agard and Grace Nichols. Copyright © 1994 by John Lyons. Reprinted by permission of Walker Books Ltd, London. Published in the U.S. by Candlewick Press, Cambridge, Massachusetts. "The Lion," by Hilaire Belloc. Reprinted by permission of the Peters Fraser & Dunlop Group Ltd. "Don't Call Alligator Long-Mouth Till You Cross River," from *Say It Again, Granny* by John Agard (Bodley Head). Reprinted by permission of Random House UK Ltd. "Mrs. Peck-Pigeon," copyright © 1951 by Eleanor Farjeon. Reprinted by permission of Harold Ober Associates Inc. and David Higham Associates. "Samuel," copyright © 1972 by Bobbi Katz. Reprinted by permission of Bobbi Katz. "Jim-Jam Pyjamas," copyright © by Gina Wilson. Reprinted by permission of Gina Wilson. "The Donkey," by Gertrude Hind. Reprinted by permission of Punch. "Oliphaunt," from *The Adventures of Tom Bombadil* by J.R.R. Tolkien. Copyright © 1962, 1990 by Unwin Hyman Ltd. Copyright © renewed 1990 by Christopher R. Tolkien, John F.R. Tolkien, and Priscilla M.A.R. Tolkien. Reprinted by permission of Houghton Mifflin Company and HarperCollins Publishers Ltd. All rights reserved. "Climbing a steep hill," by Kwaso, and "'Please don't go!' I called," by Onitsura. From *More Cricket Songs,* Japanese haiku translated by Harry Behn. Copyright © 1971 by Harry Behn. Reprinted by permission of Marian Reiner. "Firefly," by Li Po. From *A Garden of Peonies,* translated by Henry H. Hart. Copyright © 1938 by the Board of Trustees of the Leland Stanford Junior University. Copyright renewed 1966 by Henry H. Hart. Reprinted by permission of the publishers, Stanford University Press.

© This edition
Baby's First Book Club, Bristiol, PA 19907-9541

Copyright © 1997 by Kay Sproat Chorao
All rights reserved.
First published in the United States by Dutton Children's Books,
a division of Penguin Books USA Inc.
375 Hudson Street, New York, New York 10014
Designed by Sara Reynolds

Printed in USA
ISBN 1-58048-021-7

For Pam Harrison, who loves animals

MY KITTEN

Hey, my kitten, my kitten,
    And hey, my kitten, my deary!
Such a sweet pet as this
    Was neither far nor neary.

Here we go up, up, up,
    And here we go down, down, downy;
And here we go backwards and forwards,
    And here we go round, round, roundy.

Anonymous

MOON

I have a white cat whose name is Moon;
He eats catfish from a wooden spoon,
And sleeps till five each afternoon.

Moon goes out when the moon is bright
And sycamore trees are spotted white
To sit and stare in the dead of night.

Beyond still water cries a loon,
Through mulberry leaves peers a wild baboon
And in Moon's eyes I see the moon.

William Jay Smith

SONG FOR A CHILD

My kitty has a little song
She hums inside of her;
She curls up by the kitchen fire
And then begins to purr.

It sounds just like she's winding up
A tiny clock she keeps
Inside her beautiful fur coat
To wake her, when she sleeps.

Helen Bayley Davis

MONTAGUE MICHAEL

Montague Michael
You're much too fat,
You wicked old, wily old,
Well-fed cat.

All night you sleep
On a cushion of silk,
And twice a day
I bring you milk.

And once in a while,
When you catch a mouse,
You're the proudest person
In all the house.

Anonymous

THE DANCING BEAR

Oh, it's fiddle-de-dum and fiddle-de-dee,
The dancing bear ran away with me;
For the organ-grinder he came to town
With a jolly old bear in a coat of brown.
And the funny old chap joined hands with me,
While I cut a caper and so did he.
Then 'twas fiddle-de-dum and fiddle-de-dee,
I looked at him, and he winked at me,
And I whispered a word in his shaggy ear,
And I said, "I will go with you, my dear."

The dancing bear he smiled and said,
Well, he didn't say much, but he nodded his head,
As the organ-grinder began to play
"Over the hills and far away."
With a fiddle-de-dum and a fiddle-de-dee;
Oh, I looked at him and he winked at me,
And my heart was light and the day was fair,
And away I went with the dancing bear.

Oh, 'tis fiddle-de-dum and fiddle-de-dee,
The dancing bear came back with me;
For the sugar-plum trees were stripped and bare,
And we couldn't find cookies anywhere.
And the solemn old fellow he sighed and said,
Well, he didn't say much, but he shook his head,
While I looked at him and he blinked at me
Till I shed a tear and so did he;
And both of us thought of our supper that lay
Over the hills and far away.
Then the dancing bear he took my hand,
And we hurried away through the twilight land;
And 'twas fiddle-de-dum and fiddle-de-dee
When the dancing bear came back with me.

Albert Bigelow Paine

MONKEY

WHEN YOU TALK TO A MONKEY

When you talk to a monkey
He seems very wise.
He scratches his head
And he blinks both his eyes;
But he won't say a word.
He just swings on a rail
And makes a big question mark
Out of his tail.

Rowena Bennett

BROTHERS

That handsome little chimpanzee
Looks very much like you—or me!

William Cole

MONKEYS ON THE BED

Three little monkeys
Jumping on the bed;
One fell off
And knocked his head.
Momma called the doctor,
The doctor said:
"No more monkeys
Jumping on the bed."

Anonymous

MOUSE

LITTLE MISS LIMBERKIN

Little Miss Limberkin,
    Dreadful to say,
Found a mouse in the cupboard
    Sleeping away.
Little Miss Limberkin
    Gave such a scream,
She frightened the little mouse
    Out of its dream.

Mary Mapes Dodge

THE OLD WOMAN

You know that old woman
    Who lived in a shoe?
She had so many children
    She didn't know what to do?

I think if she lived in
    A little shoe-house
That little old lady was
    Surely a mouse!

Beatrix Potter

MICE

I think mice
Are rather nice.
    Their tails are long,
    Their faces small,
    They haven't any
    Chins at all.
    Their ears are pink,
    Their teeth are white,
    They run about
    The house at night.
    They nibble things
    They shouldn't touch
    And no one seems
    To like them much.
But *I* think mice
Are nice.

Rose Fyleman

SEA GULL

THE SEA GULL

I watched the pretty, white sea gull
Come riding into town;
The waves came up when he came up,
Went down when he went down.

Leroy F. Jackson

DUCK

THE PRAYER OF THE LITTLE DUCKS

Dear God,
give us a flood of water.
Let it rain tomorrow and always.
Give us plenty of little slugs
and other luscious things to eat.
Protect all folk who quack
and everyone who knows how to swim.

Amen

Carmen Bernos de Gasztold

THE DUCK

Behold the duck.
It does not cluck.
A cluck it lacks.
It quacks.
It is specially fond
Of a puddle or pond.
When it dines or sups,
It bottoms ups.

Ogden Nash

DOG

THE HAIRY DOG

My dog's so furry I've not seen
His face for years and years:
His eyes are buried out of sight,
I only guess his ears.

When people ask me for his breed,
I do not know or care:
He has the beauty of them all
Hidden beneath his hair.

Herbert Asquith

OLD SAGER

Took old Sager out a-huntin' one night,
    Blind as he could be;
He treed eleven possums up a sour gum stump,
    I'll be danged if Sager can't see.

Anonymous

TOM'S LITTLE DOG

Tom told his dog called Tim to beg,
And up at once he sat,
His two clear amber eyes fixed fast,
His haunches on his mat.

Tom poised a lump of sugar on
His nose; then, "Trust!" says he;
Stiff as a guardsman sat his Tim;
Never a hair stirred he.

"Paid for!" says Tom; and in a trice
Up jerked that moist black nose;
A snap of teeth, a crunch, a munch,
And down the sugar goes!

Walter de la Mare

DOGS

I had a little dog,
    and my dog was very small.
He licked me in the face,
    and he answered to my call.
Of all the treasures that were mine,
    I loved him best of all.

Frances Cornford

PIG

DANCE A JIG

Come dance a jig
To my granny's pig,
    With a raudy, rowdy, dowdy;
Come dance a jig
To my granny's pig,
    And pussy-cat shall crowdy.

Anonymous

I HAD A LITTLE PIG

I had a little pig,
I fed him in a trough,
He got so fat
His tail dropped off.
So I got me a hammer,
And I got me a nail,
And I made my little pig
A brand-new tail.

Anonymous

RABBIT

THE RABBIT

When they said the time to hide was mine,
I hid back under a thick grape vine.

And while I was still for the time to pass,
A little gray thing came out of the grass.

He hopped his way through the melon bed
And sat down close by a cabbage head.

He sat down close where I could see,
And his big still eyes looked hard at me,

His big eyes bursting out of the rim,
And I looked back very hard at him.

Elizabeth Madox Roberts

GRANDFATHER FROG

Fat green frog sits by the pond,
Big frog, bull frog, grandfather frog.
Croak-croak-croak.
Shuts his eye, opens his eye,
Rolls his eye, winks his eye,
Waiting for
A little fat fly.
Croak, croak.
I go walking down by the pond,
I want to see the big green frog,
I want to stare right into his eye,
Rolling, winking, funny old eye.
But oh! he hears me coming by.
Croak-croak—
SPLASH!!

Louise Seaman Bechtel

THE POLLIWOG

Oh, the Polliwog is woggling
   In his pleasant native bog
With his beady eyes a-goggling
   Through the underwater fog
And his busy tail a-joggling
   And his eager head agog—
Just a happy little frogling
   Who is bound to be a Frog!

Arthur Guiterman

TURTLE

THE LITTLE TURTLE

There was a little turtle.
He lived in a box.
He swam in a puddle.
He climbed on the rocks.

He snapped at a mosquito.
He snapped at a flea.
He snapped at a minnow.
And he snapped at me.

He caught the mosquito.
He caught the flea.
He caught the minnow.
But he didn't catch me.

Vachel Lindsay

THE PUM NA-NA FROGS

Pum na-na,"
say the frogs
on a rainy season night
when the moon is bright.

"Pum, pum, pum-na-na,
pum, pum pum-na-na."
They sit in their muddy pools
thinking
that candleflies
are shooting stars.

John Lyons

THE LION

The Lion, the Lion, he dwells in the waste,
He has a big head and a very small waist;
But his shoulders are stark, and his jaws they are grim,
And a good little child will not play with him.

Hilaire Belloc

ALLIGATOR

**DON'T CALL ALLIGATOR
LONG-MOUTH TILL
YOU CROSS RIVER**

Call alligator long-mouth
Call alligator saw-mouth
Call alligator pushy-mouth
Call alligator scissors-mouth
Call alligator raggedy-mouth
Call alligator bumpy-bum
Call alligator all dem rude word
but better wait
            till you cross river.

John Agard

CATCH HIM, CROW!

Catch him, crow! Carry him, Kate!
Take him away till the apples are ripe;
When they are ripe and ready to fall,
Here comes baby, apples and all!

Anonymous

A LITTLE COCK SPARROW

A little cock sparrow sat on a green tree,
And he chirruped, he chirruped, so merry was he.
A naughty boy came with his wee bow and arrow,
Says he, I will shoot this little cock sparrow.
His body will make me a nice little stew,
And his giblets will make me a little pie too.
Oh, no, said the sparrow, I won't make a stew,
So he clapped his wings and away he flew.

Anonymous

MRS. PECK-PIGEON

Mrs. Peck-Pigeon
Is picking for bread,
Bob-bob-bob
Goes her little round head.
Tame as a pussy cat
In the street,
Step-step-step
Go her little red feet.
With her little red feet
And her little round head,
Mrs. Peck-Pigeon
Goes picking for bread.

Eleanor Farjeon

THE SECRET

We have a secret, just we three,
The robin, and I, and the sweet cherry-tree;
The bird told the tree, and the tree told me,
And nobody knows it but just us three.

But of course the robin knows it best,
Because he built the—I shan't tell the rest;
And laid the four little—something in it—
I'm afraid I shall tell it every minute.

But if the tree and the robin don't peep,
I'll try my best the secret to keep;
Though I know when the little birds fly about
Then the whole secret will be out.

Anonymous

SEA LIFE

THE SEA

Behold the wonders of the mighty deep,
Where crabs and lobsters learn to creep,
And little fishes learn to swim,
And clumsy sailors tumble in.

Anonymous

SALAMANDER

SAMUEL

I found this salamander
Near the pond in the woods.
Samuel, I called him—
Samuel, Samuel.
Right away I loved him.
He loved me too, I think.
Samuel, I called him—
Samuel, Samuel.

I took him home in a coffee can,
And at night
He slept in my bed.
In the morning
I took him to school.

He died very quietly during spelling.

Sometimes I think
I should have left him
Near the pond in the woods.
Samuel, I called him—
Samuel, Samuel.

Bobbi Katz

JIM-JAM PYJAMAS

He wears striped jim-jam pyjamas,
You never saw jim-jams like those,
A fine-fitting, stretchy, fur cat-suit,
Skin-tight from his head to his toes.

He wears striped jim-jam pyjamas,
Black and yellow and dashingly gay;
He makes certain that everyone sees them
By keeping them on all the day.

He wears striped jim-jam pyjamas,
He walks with a smug-pussy stride;
There's no hiding his pride in his jim-jams
With their zig-zaggy lines down each side.

He wears striped jim-jam pyjamas
And pauses at times to display
The effect as he flexes his torso—
Then he fancies he hears people say:

"I wish I had jim-jam pyjamas!
I wish I were feline and slim!
Oh, look at that brave Bengal tiger!
Oh, how I should love to be him!"

Gina Wilson

DONKEY

THE DONKEY

I saw a donkey
　　One day old,
His head was too big
　　For his neck to hold;
His legs were shaky
　　And long and loose,
They rocked and staggered
　　And weren't much use.
He tried to gambol
　　And frisk a bit,
But he wasn't quite sure
　　Of the trick of it.
His queer little coat
　　Was soft and grey
And curled at his neck
　　In a lovely way.

His face was wistful
　　And left no doubt
That he felt life needed
　　Some thinking out.
So he blundered round
　　In venturous quest,
And then lay flat
　　On the ground to rest.
He looked so little
　　And weak and slim,
I prayed the world
　　Might be good to him.

Gertrude Hind

HORSE

RIDING TO MARKET

Ride a cock-horse to Coventry Cross,
To see what Emma can buy;
A penny white cake I'll buy for her sake,
And a twopenny apple pie.

Anonymous

I HAD A LITTLE HORSE

I had a little horse,
His name was Dapple Gray,
His head was made of gingerbread,
His tail was made of hay.
He could amble, he could trot,
He could carry the mustard pot.

Anonymous

ELEPHANT

OLIPHAUNT

Grey as a mouse,
Big as a house,
Nose like a snake,
I make the earth shake,
As I tramp through the grass;
Trees crack as I pass.
With horns in my mouth
I walk in the South,
Flapping big ears.
Beyond count of years
I stump round and round,
Never lie on the ground,
Not even to die.
Oliphaunt am I,
Biggest of all,
Huge, old, and tall.
If ever you'd met me,
You wouldn't forget me.
If you never do,
You won't think I'm true;
But old Oliphaunt am I,
And I never lie.

J.R.R. Tolkien

I ASKED MY MOTHER

I asked my mother for fifty cents
To see the elephant jump the fence.
He jumped so high that he touched the sky
And never came back till the Fourth of July.

Anonymous

L A M B

from SPRING

Little lamb,
Here I am;
Come and lick
My white neck;
Let me pull
Your soft wool;
Let me kiss
Your soft face;
Merrily, merrily, we welcome in the year.

William Blake

GOAT

BILLY GOAT

There was a young goat named Billy
Who was more than a little bit silly.
They sent him to school
But he just played the fool
And ate satchels and books willy-nilly.

Anonymous

BUTTERFLY

Climbing a steep hill
I saw below, on a tree's
top twig, a butterfly.

Kwaso

from TO A BUTTERFLY

I've watched you now a full half-hour,
Self-pois'd upon that yellow flower;
And, little Butterfly, indeed
I know not if you sleep or feed.

How motionless!—not frozen seas
More motionless; and then
What joy awaits you, when the breeze
Hath found you out among the trees,
And calls you forth again!

William Wordsworth

FIREFLY

Although the night is damp,
The little firefly ventures out,
And slowly lights his lamp.

Anonymous

from
FIREFLY

I think
if you flew
up to the sky
beside the moon,
you would
twinkle
like a star.

Li Po

Please don't go!" I called,
but the fireflies flashed away
deep into darkness.

Onitsura

KANGAROO

THE KANGAROO

Old Jumpety-Bumpety-Hop-and-Go-One
Was lying asleep on his side in the sun.
This old kangaroo, he was whisking the flies
(With his long glossy tail) from his ears and his eyes.
Jumpety-Bumpety-Hop-and-Go-One
Was lying asleep on his side in the sun,
Jumpety-Bumpety-Hop!

Anonymous

OSTRICH

HERE IS THE OSTRICH

Here is the ostrich straight and tall,
Nodding his head above us all.

Here is the long snake on the ground,
Wriggling on the stones around.

Here are the birds that fly so high,
Spreading their wings across the sky.

Here is the bushrat, furry and small,
Rolling himself into a ball.

Here is the spider scuttling round,
Treading so lightly on the ground.

Here are the children fast asleep,

And here at night the owls do peep.

Anonymous

Index